D1194067

Sara Swan Miller

Cicadas and Aphids

What They Have in Common

Franklin Watts · A Division of Grolier Publishing
New York • London • Hong Kong • Sydney • Danbury, Connecticut

For Betty McKnight, who introduced me to
the world of Outdoor Environmental Education

j595.752
M618c

Photographs ©: Animals Animals: 33 (C.W. Perkins); Edward S. Ross: 21, 35, 39; Frederick D. Atwood: 37; Jack K. Clark: 5 top right, 5 bottom right, 19, 23, 27, 31; Photo Researchers: 43 (Perennon et Nuridsany), 5 top left (Scott Camazine), 25 (Holt Studios Int.), 5 bottom left (Stephen J. Krasemann); Steve Marshall: 40, 13, 29; Visuals Unlimited: 41 (Bill Beatty), cover, 15 (Tom Edwards), 1 (R. Lindholm), 17 (Joe McDonald), 6 (D. Newman), 42 (John Sohlden), 7 (Richard Walters).

Illustrations by Jose Gonzales and Steve Savage

Visit Franklin Watts on the Internet at:
http://publishing.grolier.com

Library of Congress Cataloging-in-Publication Data

Miller, Sara Swan.
Cicadas and aphids: what they have in common / Sara Swan Miller.
    p. cm. — (Animals in order)
    Includes bibliographical references (p.) and index.
    Summary: Provides an overview of the characteristics and natural habitat of homopterans, a taxinomic order of insects that includes cicadas, aphids, scale insects, and whiteflies. Also includes advice for finding, catching, and observing this group of insects.
    ISBN 0-531-11519-4 (lib. bdg.)   0-531-15944-2 (pbk.)
    1. Homoptera—Juvenile literature   [1. Hemopterans. 2. Insects] I. Title.   II. Series.
QL525.M55   1999
595.7'52—dc21   98-2703
                                                                          CIP
                                                                          AC

© 1999 Franklin Watts
All rights reserved. Published simultaneously in Canada.
Printed in the United States of America.

GROLIER
PUBLISHING   1 2 3 4 5 6 7 8 9 10 R 08 07 06 05 04 03 02 01 00 99

Contents

ƆꝢɥᴑ

Central Childrens Department

Who Are the Homopterans?

"Look at that enormous, red-eyed bug!"
"What are all these flies doing on my houseplants?"
"Those are the smallest grasshoppers I've ever seen!"

Have you ever heard people say things like that? Were they really looking at bugs, flies, and grasshoppers? Maybe not. Not all insects are bugs, not all flying insects are flies, and not all hopping insects are grasshoppers. Those insects could have belonged to a special group called the homopterans.

Look at the insects on the next page. Even though they look quite different, they are all homopterans. Can you tell what they all have in common?

Cicada

Aphids

Spittlebug

Whitefly

Traits of the Homopterans

Like flies, all homopterans have thin, transparent wings. But most homopterans have two pairs of wings, while flies have only one pair. And homopterans usually hold their wings slanting over their body, like a little roof. The inner edges of their wings overlap. Some *species* of female homopterans have no wings. In other species, one generation has wings, but the next generation does not.

All homopterans have sucking mouthparts, which they use to slurp up plant juices. A homopteran's *beak* is attached to the rear of its head. Sometimes it seems to grow out from between the insect's front legs.

Like all homopterans, this cicada has two sets of transparent wings.

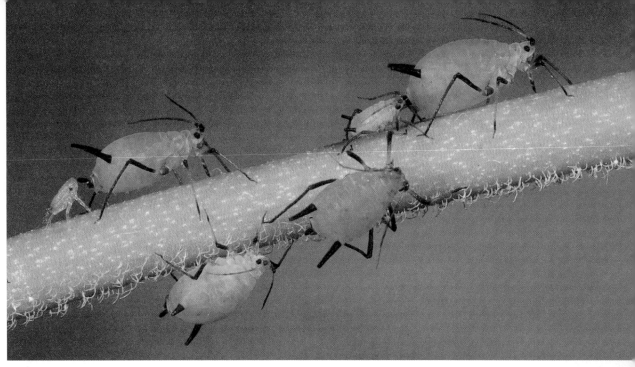

Aphid nymphs and adults look very similar.

Newly hatched homopterans are called *nymphs*. They usually look just like their parents, but they are smaller and wingless. As a nymph grows, it sheds its outer layer several times. It quickly replaces this skinlike layer, called an *exoskeleton*, with a larger one. Its wings get longer each time the nymph sheds.

Most homopterans mate to produce young, but aphids are an exception to this rule. Aphids can produce many generations without mating. While most homopterans lay eggs, some give birth to live young.

There are thousands and thousands of different species of homopterans in the world. They live in all kinds of places—in fields and gardens, in woods and orchards, and even in the desert. Some may be living in your home right now, sucking away at your delicious houseplants.

The Order of Living Things

A tiger has more in common with a house cat than with a daisy. A true bug is more like a butterfly than a jellyfish. Scientists arrange living things into groups based on how they look and how they act. A tiger and a house cat belong to the same group, but a daisy belongs to a different group.

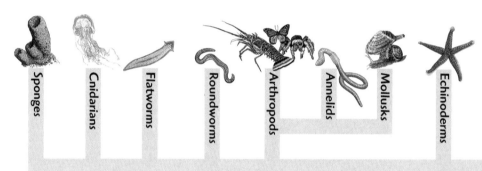

Sponges · Cnidarians · Flatworms · Roundworms · Arthropods · Annelids · Mollusks · Echinoderms

Animals

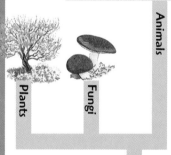

Plants · Fungi

Protists

Monerans

All living things can be placed in one of five groups called *kingdoms*: the plant kingdom, the animal kingdom, the fungus kingdom, the moneran kingdom, or the protist kingdom. You can probably name many of the creatures in the plant and animal kingdoms. The fungus kingdom includes mushrooms, yeasts, and molds. The moneran and protist kingdoms contain thousands of living things that are too small to see without a microscope.

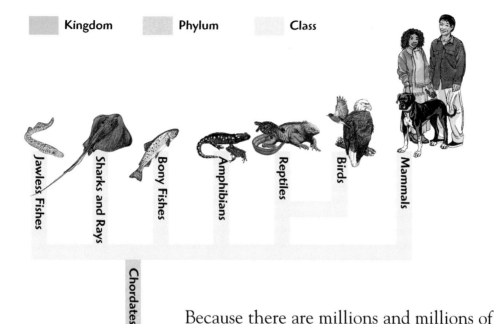

Kingdom Phylum Class

Jawless Fishes

Sharks and Rays

Bony Fishes

Amphibians

Reptiles

Birds

Mammals

Chordates

Because there are millions and millions of living things on Earth, some of the members of one kingdom may not seem all that similar. The animal kingdom includes creatures as different as tarantulas and trout, jellyfish and jaguars, salamanders and sparrows, elephants and earthworms.

To show that an elephant is more like a jaguar than an earthworm, scientists further separate the creatures in each kingdom into more specific groups. The animal kingdom can be divided into nine *phyla*. Humans belong to the chordate phylum. Almost all chordates have a backbone.

Each phylum can be subdivided into many *classes*. Humans, mice, and elephants all belong to the mammal class. Each class can be further divided into *orders*; orders into *families*, families into *genera*, and genera into species. All the members of a species are very similar.

How Homopterans Fit In

You can probably guess that the homopterans belong to the animal kingdom. They have much more in common with spiders and snakes than with maple trees and morning glories.

Homopterans belong to the arthropod phylum. All arthropods have a tough outer skin. Can you guess what other living things might be arthropods? Examples include spiders, scorpions, mites, ticks, millipedes, and centipedes. Some arthropods live in the ocean. Lobsters, crabs, and shrimps all belong to this group.

The arthropod phylum can be divided into a number of classes. Homopterans belong to the insect class. Butterflies, ants, flies, and beetles are also insects.

There are thirty different orders of insects. The homopterans make up one of these orders. The word "homoptera" means "similar wings." As you learned earlier, the wings of homopterans are transparent from the base to the tip.

The homopterans can be divided into a number of different families and genera. These groups can be broken down into thousands of species. You will learn more about some of the homopterans in this book.

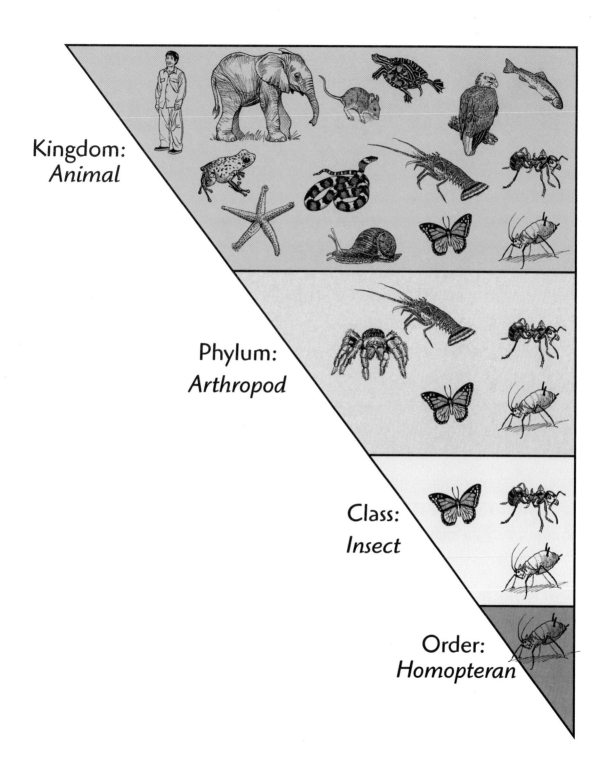

Kingdom:
Animal

Phylum:
Arthropod

Class:
Insect

Order:
Homopteran

Periodical Cicadas

FAMILY: Cicadidae
COMMON EXAMPLE: Seventeen-year cicada
GENUS AND SPECIES: *Magicicada septendecim*
SIZE: 1 1/8 inch (28.5 mm)

Can you imagine spending the first 17 years of your life underground? That is exactly what 17-year cicadas do. They build a network of tunnels and live by sucking on the juices of plant roots until they grow into adults. Just think, thousands of cicadas could be living under your feet right now!

In late spring—all at once and all together—the cicadas emerge from their tunnels. Then the ground is alive with cicadas! They climb up tree trunks and shed their skins for the last time. Out come thousands of big red-eyed adults ready to mate. Then males start calling for the females in loud, whining voices. The combined whining of thousands of cicadas can be almost deafening!

Seventeen-year cicadas enjoy life aboveground for only a few weeks. After mating, the females lay their eggs in slits they have made in tree branches, and then all the adults die. A few weeks later, the young hatch and drop to the ground. They dig into the *soil* with their big, powerful front legs. And there they stay for 17 long, dark years.

While the nymphs are underground, they are safe from most enemies. When they finally emerge, there are so many of them that birds can't possibly eat them all. Cicadas are smarter than you think!

Annual Cicadas

FAMILY: Cicadidae
COMMON EXAMPLE: Dog day harvestfly
GENUS AND SPECIES: *Tibicen canicularis*
SIZE: 1 1/8 to 1 1/4 inches (28.5 to 32 mm)

What is that awful noise? Is someone using a circular saw? It's hard to believe that one tiny insect could make such an ear-piercing sound.

Male cicadas are the loudest insects on Earth. Each one has a complex sound-making device inside its body. When the cicada contracts and expands a large muscle in its *abdomen*, internal membranes vibrate. These vibrations are then transmitted to other membranes that act like the amplifiers a rock band uses. Just think how loud that can be!

Every year, during the "dog days" of summer, you can hear the constant calls of dog day harvest flies searching for mates. The adults are so busy that they hardly ever stop to eat. When they do, they suck on sap from twigs. After the females lay their eggs in tree branches, all the adults die. When the nymphs hatch, they burrow into the ground and stay there for 3 years. During that time, they suck on roots to build up strength for their moment in the sun.

Cicadas have many enemies, including gulls, grackles, and crows. They have to watch out for people, too. In the South Pacific, some people gather the largest to munch on. Delicious!

Treehoppers

FAMILY: Membracidae
COMMON EXAMPLE: Thorn mimic treehopper
GENUS AND SPECIES: *Campylenchia latipes*
SIZE: 1/4 inch (6 mm)

If you live in California, take a close look at a thorn tree sometime. If you watch carefully and wait patiently, you may see something strange. One of the thorns might move!

What you are seeing isn't really a thorn at all, it's a type of treehopper called the thorn mimic. Part of this insect's exoskeleton grows into a hard, thorn-shaped structure. If you flap your hand at the tree, the thorn mimics will hop away in all directions.

Most of the time, thorn mimics stay perfectly still while they suck the thorn tree juices. This behavior fools birds and other enemies. After all, who wants to eat a thorn?

In eastern North America, you may be able to spot gray-and-yellow locust treehoppers on *locust trees*. Also be on the lookout for brightly colored buffalo treehoppers. They are yellow and green— and they look as though they are sporting a pair of buffalo horns.

Some of the treehoppers that live close to the equator look even stranger. One species has a huge crescent-shaped flap on its back, while another has a large arched flap. It's a wonder these treehoppers can hop at all. Carrying all that extra baggage must make it hard to move.

Armored Scale Insects

FAMILY: Diaspididae
COMMON EXAMPLE: Purple scale
GENUS AND SPECIES: *Lepidosaphes beckii*
SIZE: Female 1/8 inch (3 mm)

Have you ever seen purple scales clustered on a tree branch? Maybe you didn't realize they were insects. That's because they hide themselves under a disk, or scale, made of old, cast-off skins glued together with wax.

The adult female never moves. She can't move because she has no legs! She has no eyes or antennae, either. All she does is suck tree juices and lay eggs. The adult male does have legs, antennae, and wings, so it is his job to find a female and mate with her. In some species, the female doesn't even need to mate in order to give birth.

The purple scale female lays her eggs in the fall. After the frost kills her, the tough scale that covers her body stays attached to the tree and protects her eggs all winter long. When the nymphs hatch, they crawl around for a few hours in search of a good spot to settle down. Then they pierce the tree bark and start sucking the tree juices. Soon, a scale forms over them, too.

Fruit growers do not like purple scales because these insects eat crops. They are very successful pests because once their scales have formed, birds and other *predators* can't eat them. And one female scale insect can produce thousands of young in a single year!

18

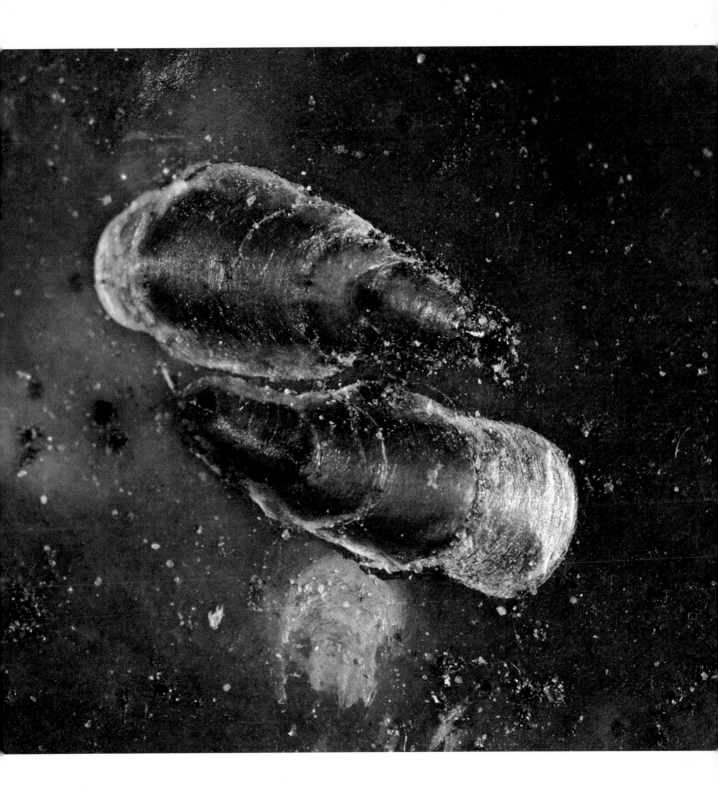

19

Giant Scale Insects

FAMILY: Margarodidae
COMMON EXAMPLE: Cottony cushion scale
GENUS AND SPECIES: *Icerya purchasi*
SIZE: Female 1/8 to 1/4 inch (3 to 6 mm);
Male 1/16 inch (1.5 mm)

Like armored scale insects, giant scale insects hide under waxy scales. The wingless females stay in one place all their lives, sucking on plant juices. Only the males can fly around.

Some of these insects are quite beautiful. In southern parts of the world, some species are covered with shiny bronze- or gold-colored scales. People call them "ground pearls" and use the scales to create jewelry.

You can recognize a female because she has an egg sac attached to her body. Out of this sac come 600 to 1,000 brightly colored young. At first, they suck leaf juices. Later, they slurp the juices from twigs while they hide in their waxy homes. Like moths, male scales spin cocoons and stay inside them while they grow into adults. The females come out from under their protective disk and *molt* in the open.

Cottony cushion scales were accidentally transported from Australia to the United States in the 1800s. Because they have no natural predators in North America, these insects spread quickly and devastated many orchards. Farmers were worried. There seemed to be

20

no solution to this terrible problem? Then someone had a bright idea. Why not import Australian ladybird beetles—the cottony cushion scale's worst enemy. It didn't take long for the hungry beetles to gobble up enough scales to save North America's orchards.

Woolly Aphids

FAMILY: Eriosomatidae
COMMON EXAMPLE: Woolly apple aphid
GENUS AND SPECIES: *Eriosoma lanigerum*
SIZE: 1/16 inch (1.5 mm)

For a simple-looking insect, the woolly apple aphid has a very complicated *life cycle*. In late summer, a winged female flies to an *elm tree*, mates with a male, and lays a single egg deep in a crevice in the bark. When the egg hatches in the spring, a wingless female nymph emerges.

The nymph grows into an adult that can lay eggs without mating. Out of those eggs hatch more wingless females, who also lay eggs without mating. The females that hatch from these eggs grow into winged adults. They fly until they find an apple tree and lay eggs— again without the help of a mate—in the tree's roots. The nymphs that hatch from these eggs grow, again, into wingless female adults. And they produce another generation of wingless, non-mating females.

Finally, in late summer, winged females develop from the eggs laid by the wingless, non-mating females. Each of these aphids flies to an elm tree, mates with a male, and lays a single egg in the elm tree bark. Then the whole complicated cycle starts all over again.

Woolly apple aphids are usually purple and are covered with hairs of cottony wax. When large numbers of these insects live on the

same tree, it looks as though it is covered with cotton. The hairs probably keep the woolly aphids warm, just like a sheep's wool.

Apple growers don't like these aphids very much, but they have learned an easy way to control these insects. They just make sure there are no elm trees near their orchards.

Psyllids

FAMILY: Psyllidae
COMMON EXAMPLE: Apple sucker psyllid
GENUS AND SPECIES: *Psylla mali*
SIZE: 1/16 to 1/8 inch (1 to 3 mm)

You have to be a real nature detective to get to know the psyllids. These homopterans are really tiny and blend well with their surroundings. To spot apple sucker psyllids, grab a hand lens and find apple trees growing near a stream or lake.

In the early spring, look for the tiny, pale yellow eggs on the bark. The nymphs hatch just as the new leaves begin to open. The young nymphs are flat, oval, and bright green. Older nymphs, which hatched in the fall and spent the winter under the bark, are larger and darker.

Soon, last year's nymphs turn into adults. These adults look quite different from the nymphs. They have transparent wings with rounded ends. If you look closely, you might think they look like tiny cicadas. Like cicadas, and all other homopterans, psyllids feed on plant juices.

Try to get a good look at a psyllid's legs. They don't look like the legs of other jumping insects. But if you brush one with a leaf, you will see just how well these tiny insects can hop!

Leafhoppers

FAMILY: Cicadellidae
COMMON EXAMPLE: Variegated grape leafhopper
GENUS AND SPECIES: *Erythroneura variabilis*
SIZE: 1/16 to 1/8 inch (1.5 to 3 mm)

Leafhoppers are very common insects, but they are so tiny that you have probably never noticed them. And while many leafhoppers are brightly colored, most of them blend well with their surroundings.

If an enemy threatens a leafhopper, it can use its powerful hind legs to leap away. It may also dart around to the other side of the leaf it is feeding on. After a few moments, the leafhopper will run back to see if the predator has gone. If not, the leafhopper darts away again. You can see why some people call these insects "dodgers."

Other people call leafhoppers "sharpshooters." Watch one feeding, and you will soon understand why. As a leafhopper eats, it shoots tiny drops of clear liquid from its tail. Where does the liquid come from? The plant juices it sucks on go through the leafhopper's body so quickly that they are hardly digested before shooting out the other end. Flies, ants, bees, and other insects love the sugary taste of this liquid. That's why you often see groups of insects crowding around a colony of leafhoppers.

Variegated grape leafhoppers eat more than just grape leaves. They also like berries, maple trees, plum trees, and many other plants. Maybe that's why there are so many of these little leapers.

Spittlebugs

FAMILY: Cercopidae
COMMON EXAMPLE: Meadow spittlebug
GENUS AND SPECIES: *Philaenus spumarius*
SIZE: 3/8 inch (9.5 mm)

Have you ever walked across a meadow and seen blobs of what looked like spit on blades of grass? If you had looked inside one of those blobs, you would have found a meadow spittlebug nymph hiding there.

As soon as it hatches, a spittlebug nymph hangs upside down on a plant stem, so that a clear liquid can flow out of its tail down over its body. As the liquid covers the spittlebug's body, the nymph blows air into it. The air shooting out of the spittlebug's body acts like an egg-beater—it whips the liquid into a froth.

The nymph is safe inside its frothy home. No bird is going to stick its beak into that uninviting ball of spit, and other insects have no idea there's anything good to eat inside it. The froth also prevents the nymph from drying out in the sun.

Once the nymph has grown into an adult, it doesn't need to hide in its ball of froth anymore. Because spittlebugs are the same shade of gray or green as the plants they feed on, birds don't notice them. If a larger insect attacks, the spittlebug hops out of sight.

Adult spittlebugs don't just hop like frogs—they also look like tiny tree frogs. Some people even call them "froghoppers."

Aphids

FAMILY: Aphididae
COMMON EXAMPLE: Potato aphid
GENUS AND SPECIES: *Macrosiphum euphorbiae*
SIZE: 1/8 inch (3 mm)

Aphids are tiny, weak insects with soft bodies and such thin, puny legs that they can hardly walk. Many aphids are wingless, and those that do have wings are feeble fliers. It's a wonder they can even survive. Yet aphids thrive all over the world. What is their secret?

Aphids have many generations of young each year. Potato aphids lay their eggs on rosebushes in the fall. When the nymphs hatch, they feed on the rosebush. Later in the summer, you can find them on apple trees, potatoes, eggplant, corn, and flowers.

As an aphid sucks on plant juices, a sweet liquid called *honeydew* flows from its tail. Some species of ants love the sweet juice so much that they "farm" aphids, just as we farm dairy cows. If other insects attack their aphids, the ants fight to the death to protect their herd.

These farming ants do more than protect aphids from enemies. Many build shelters for their aphids or take them into their nests in bad weather. Some ants gather aphid eggs and take them into their nests in the fall and protect them all winter long. In the spring, the ants carry the eggs back to the place where they were laid. Some ants even transport their aphid herds to fresh "pastures" when the food supply runs low.

31

Whiteflies

FAMILY: Aleyrodidae
COMMON EXAMPLE: Greenhouse whitefly
GENUS AND SPECIES: *Trialeurodes vaporariorum*
SIZE: 1/16 inch (1.5 mm)

Have you ever noticed tiny white specks on your houseplants? You may have thought that your plants were getting awfully dusty. But if you look closely at those specks of "dust" with a hand lens, you will see that they are actually tiny homopterans called whiteflies. The paddle-shaped wings of adult whiteflies make these insects look like little white moths covered with powder.

Whitefly nymphs are flat and oval. They attach themselves to leaves with the waxy, white strands that cover their bodies. Looking like a piece of lint is a good way to fool an enemy!

The nymphs grow and molt, grow and molt until they reach adulthood. Most homopterans do not go through a resting stage. But the growth cycle of a whitefly nymph is more like that of a moth or a butterfly. The nymph looks quite different from the adult. Just before it molts for the last time, the nymph rests inside its last skin, like a caterpillar in a cocoon. When the whitefly comes out, it is a winged adult.

Greenhouse whiteflies have spread all over the world. In warmer regions, they live outdoors. But northern winters are too cold for whiteflies to survive. Luckily, they can spend the winter in nice, warm greenhouses with plenty of delicious plants to feed on!

33

Mealybugs

FAMILY: Pseudocioccidae
COMMON EXAMPLE: Long-tailed mealybug
GENUS AND SPECIES: *Pseudococcus adonidum*
SIZE: 1/16 to 1/8 inch (1.5 to 3 mm)

Maybe those tiny white specks on your houseplants aren't really whiteflies. They could be mealybugs. These tiny, oval insects are hidden under a covering of white wax that keeps them safe from most of their enemies.

If you look closely at a long-tailed mealybug, you might think it looks like a fat, many-legged millipede with extra tails. But those "legs" are really little spines. Like other insects, a mealybug has only six legs.

Mealybugs seem to enjoy company. They flock together like sheep to suck on plant juices. You may notice ants flocking around them, too. Like their cousins the aphids, mealybugs give out sweet honeydew that the ants love. Ants will fight to the death to protect their mealybugs from ladybugs and other enemies.

Female long-tailed mealybugs give birth to live nymphs. Like other homopterans, the nymphs grow and molt several times, constantly sucking on plant juices. But in the last stage of development, male mealybugs behave more like moths and butterflies than most homopterans. They spin silken shelters to rest in. Hidden away in their cocoons, they are changing secretly. Before you know it, out comes a tiny, winged adult. Each mealybug uncurls his antennae, dries his wings, and flies off to find a female and start a new mealybug colony.

Cochineal Insects

FAMILY: Dactylopiidae
COMMON EXAMPLE: Cochinealbug
GENUS AND SPECIES: *Dactylopius confusus*
SIZE: Female 1/16 to 1/8 inch (1.5 to 3 mm)

Thousands of years ago, the Aztec people of Mexico discovered tiny red insects, hidden under a cottony wax covering, feeding on cactuses. They also discovered a way to use these insects. They brushed them off the cactuses, killed and dried them, and then ground them into powder. When they mixed the powder with liquid, the result was a beautiful red dye.

The Aztecs used the dye to decorate their temples. If you visit the ruins today, you can still see traces of those red patterns on the walls. It took about 70,000 cochinealbugs to make just 1 pound (453 g) of dye!

After the Aztecs, other groups of people discovered cochinealbugs. Native Americans in the southwestern United States used a dye made from these insects to decorate clothes and rugs. In other parts of the world, people cultivated them like a crop. They used the dye in beverages, medicines, and cosmetics. In recent years, people have started using synthetic dyes rather than those made from cochinealbugs. Harvesting and drying thousands of cochineals is too much work!

Cochinealbugs act a lot like scale insects. They cover themselves under a waxy covering, and the female doesn't move after her first molt. She lays her eggs under her scale, and then she dies. When the

36

nymphs hatch, they crawl out from under her dead body and begin sucking on cactus juice. After their first molt, they are hidden under their own little wax covers.

Lac Insects

FAMILY: Lacciferidae
COMMON EXAMPLE: Creosote bush lac scale
GENUS AND SPECIES: *Tachardiella larrae*
SIZE: 1/8 inch (3 mm)

Native Americans in the southwestern United States also discovered a use for lac insects. Both the females and nymphs are covered with a shell of hard, sticky resin that has two important functions. The resin holds them fast to the twigs they feed on, and it protects them from birds and other predators. However, resin does not protect them from humans. In fact, people collected the resin shells, killing the insects at the same time.

After gathering the resin shells of hundreds of creosote bush lac scales, Native Americans melted them down into shellac. When they painted the shellac on closely woven baskets, the baskets could hold water.

People in other parts of the world used the shells of other species of lac insects. In Asian forests, female lac insects crowd together and cover themselves with a layer of resin up to 1/2 inch (13 mm) thick. People gathered this resin, melted it down, shaped it into flakes, and mixed it with alcohol to make shellac.

For centuries, people in many parts of world used shellac to cover and protect furniture. It has also been used in ink, buttons, toys, pottery, floor coverings, sealing wax, and many other products.

But because it takes the resin from about 150,000 lac insects to make just 1 pound (453 g) of shellac, most people now rely on artificial shellac made from plastics.

Looking for Homopterans

The next time you go into the woods or out in a field, why not go on a homopteran hunt? Be sure to take along a journal so you can draw pictures of what you find and write down what you discover. If you are a good nature detective, you may find out something about homopterans that nobody has noticed before. You could become a homopteran expert!

Useful Tools

A plastic hand lens

A stopwatch or a watch with a second hand

A tape measure

A journal

A field guide to insects

A field guide to trees

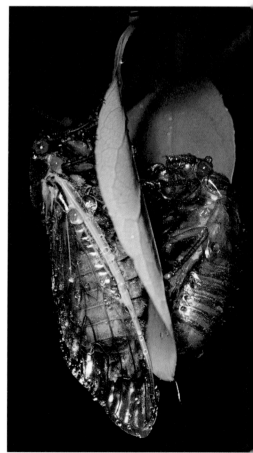

This cicada has just molted.

If you're out in the woods during the summer, listen for annual cicadas calling for their mates. Cicadas are often high in the trees, so you may not see them, but you can't miss their ear-piercing buzz. Use your watch to time how long each call lasts. You can also try to time how long one insect waits between calls. How many times does the cicada call in the space of 10 minutes? Try listening for annual cicadas at different times of the day.

When are you most likely to hear them—morning, afternoon, or evening?

You're lucky if you happen to be around when the 17-year cicadas emerge from the ground. Look for their cast-off skins on tree trunks. You may even see one wriggling out of its skin. How many cast-off skins can you find on a single tree-trunk? Write down what you find out and draw pictures of what you see.

You may also want to look for tree-hoppers. If you live in the southwestern part of the United States, look for thorn mimic treehoppers on thorn trees. In other places, look for the gray and yellow locust treehoppers or green and yellow buffalo treehoppers on locust trees. If you find some, look at them closely with a hand lens. Can you see their tiny mouths? Watch one for a while. Do you see it feeding on the tree? How long can it stay completely still? What happens if you flap your hand at it?

A treehopper

If you can find a grove of apple trees, you may find apple sucker psyllids. In early spring, look for their tiny yellow eggs on the bark. Later in the spring, you may find bright green nymphs. Do you see any adult psyllids? They look like tiny cicadas. Use a hand lens to get a closer look at what you find. Try brushing a psyllid with a leaf to see how high it jumps. Write down everything you notice in your journal.

41

All kinds of trees may have scale insects living on them. Look for them on branches. How many scale insects can you find on a single branch? Do different trees have different kinds of scale insects? In early spring, you may see the newly hatched nymphs of armored scale insects looking for a good place to settle down. You may also see the bright red nymphs of giant scale insects or a female with her cottony egg sac.

Oyster-shell scale insects on a birch tree

Look for woolly aphids in trees, particularly elm trees and apple trees. A tree full of woolly aphids may look as if it is covered with cotton. Depending on the time of year, you may find wingless adults, winged adults, or nymphs. Try to get a close-up look with a hand lens. Can you see their tiny mouths? What are they doing? Do you see them sucking on the tree juice? Do they move around a lot or stay still?

You can find colonies of aphids on all kinds of plants—potatoes, eggplants, apple trees, rosebushes, and many different kinds of flowers. When you find a colony, you will probably find ants tending them. Do you see the ants lapping the honeydew? Describe what you see in your journal. Look at the leaves the aphids are feeding on. Do you see the sticky honeydew they leave behind? Do you see black

mold growing on the leaf? This mold lives off the honeydew. If you're very patient, you may see a ladybug or another predator try to eat the aphids. Then you can watch how the fierce ants rise up to protect their herd.

Look on the leaves of shrubs, vines, berry bushes, and small maple trees for tiny leafhoppers. If you find one, watch it for a while. Can you see juice shooting out of its tail?

In a meadow, look for gobs of spit on the grass. Is a spittlebug nymph hiding inside? Use a hand lens to get a closer look. Draw what you see in your journal. You may see adult spittlebugs hopping around in the grass. They look like tiny frogs. Watch them for a while. Do you see them feeding? What happens when you startle them?

If you keep watching for homopterans, and record everything you see in your journal, you can create your own homopteran book!

Words to Know

abdomen—the third and last section of an insect's body.

beak—the portion of an insect's head that contains its mouthparts.

class—a group of creatures within a phylum that share certain characteristics.

elm tree—tree with double-toothed, feather-veined leaves, and grayish ridged bark.

exoskeleton—the hard, skinlike outer shell of insects and other arthropods.

family—a group of creatures within an order that share certain characteristics.

genus (plural genera)—a group of creatures within a family that share certain characteristics.

habitat—the environment where a plant or animal lives and grows.

honeydew—a sweet fluid released by aphids and some other homopterans. In some cases, other insects feed on honeydew.

kingdom—one of the five divisions into which all living things are placed: the animal kingdom, the plant kingdom, the fungus kingdom, the moneran kingdom, and the protist kingdom.

life cycle—the stages of a creature's life.

locust tree—a tree with feather-compound leaves with numerous narrow leaflets, and with branched thorns on its bark.

molt—to shed and regrow an exoskeleton. Most insects and other arthropods molt several times before becoming adults.

nymph—a young homopteran. This name is used until the insect undergoes metamorphosis and becomes an adult.

order—a group of organisms within a class that share certain characteristics.

phylum (plural **phyla**)—a group of creatures within a kingdom that share certain characteristics.

predator—an animal that catches and feeds on other animals.

soil—the mixture of decaying plant matter and broken-down rocks that covers the land portion of Earth's surface.

species—a group of organisms within a genus that share certain characteristics. Members of a species can mate and produce young.

Learning More

Books

Booth, Jerry. *Big Bugs*. San Diego: Harcourt Brace, 1994.

Ganeri, Anita. *Insects*. New York: Franklin Watts, 1993.

Leahy, Christopher. *Peterson's First Guide to Insects*. Boston: Houghton Mifflin, 1987.

Mound, Laurence. *Amazing Insects*. New York: Alfred A. Knopf, 1993.

Silver, Donald A. *One Small Square: Backyard*. New York: W.H. Freeman and Co., 1995.

CD-ROM

Bug Adventure: An Insect Adventure. Knowledge Adventure, 1995.

Videos

Insect. Eyewitness Video Series.

Insects: Little Things that Run the World. NOVA Video Library.

Web Sites

The Bug Club Page has a list of insect experts that you can contact by e-mail. The club also organizes local field trips and publishes a newsletter six times a year.
http://www.ex.ac.uk/bugclub

The Young Entomologist's Society Page runs a program called "Bugs-On-Wheels." You may be able to arrange for an insect expert to visit your school and show your classmates some really cool insects.
http://insects.ummz.lsa.umich.edu/yes/yes.html

Index

About the Author

Sara Swan Miller has enjoyed working with children all her life, first as a Montessori nursery school teacher, and later as an outdoor environmental educator at the Mohonk Preserve in New Paltz, New York. As the director of the Preserve school program, she has led hundreds of children on field trips and taught them the importance of appreciating and respecting the natural world, especially its less lovable "creepy crawlies."

She has written a number of children's books including *Three Stories You Can Read to Your Dog*; *Three Stories You Can Read to Your Cat*; *What's in the Woods?: An Outdoor Activity Book*; *Oh, Cats of Camp Rabbitbone*; *Piggy in the Parlor and Other Tales*; *Better Than TV*; and *Will You Sting Me? Will You Bite?: The Truth About Some Scary-Looking Insects*. She has also written several other books in the Animals in Order series.

Central Childrens Department

6/00

27 4/15
25 3/14
13 7/09
12 4/05
8 5/01